Extremely WEIRD

ANIMAL DEFENSES

Text by Sarah Lovett

John Muir Publications
Santa Fe, New Mexico

John Muir Publications, P.O. Box 613, Santa Fe, New Mexico 87504

First edition. First printing March 1997.

Library of Congress Cataloging-in-Publication Data
Lovett, Sarah, 1953–
    Animal defenses / text by Sarah Lovett.
        p.   cm. — (Extremely weird)
    Includes index.
    Summary: Describes the physical characteristics and behavior of
a number of animals with unusual means of defense, including the burrfish,
the gelada, and the bulldog ant.
    ISBN 1-56261-358-8
    1. Animal defenses—Juvenile literature. [1. Animal defenses.]
    I. Title. II. Series: Lovett, Sarah, 1953– Extremely weird.
QL759.L68 1997
591.47—dc21   96-40014
                                                      CIP
                                                      AC

Extremely Weird Logo Art: Peter Aschwanden
Illustrations: Mary Sundstrom, Sally Blakemore
Design: Sally Blakemore
Typography: Copygraphics, Inc., Santa Fe, New Mexico
Printer: Burton & Mayer, Inc.

Distributed to the book trade by
Publishers Group West
Emeryville, California

Cover photo: Bulldog ant, courtesy Animals Animals/Oxford Scientific Films © Kathie Atkinson

I N T R O D U C T I O N

The Animal Kingdom is a brutal world—every day its inhabitants face the threat of being eaten. Only the most fit, the most cunning, and the most creative survive. The weak defend themselves from the strong. The hunted, called prey, defend themselves from the hunters, called predators.

Over millions of years, in order to prevent the extinction of their species, many animals have evolved unique defenses against predators. Animals defend themselves with armor, smelly scents, fast legs, and strong wings. Some use disguises, or camouflage, to blend into their surroundings and hide from their predators. Some animals, such as the sea cucumber, use a poisonous skin to discourage predators. Others, like the burrfish, try to scare hungry predators away by making themselves look bigger and more fierce than they really are. Still others, such as the African porcupine, have sharp spines or hairs that spoil the appetites of even the toughest predators. Senses are also very important for animal defense. An acute sense of smell can warn an animal that a predator is nearby. Some animals have learned to attack the attacker—with sharp teeth and claws. When all else fails, animals stamp their feet, swing their tusks, fan their frills, throw rocks, or just curl up and hide—anything to survive.

Turn to the glossarized index at the back of the book if you're looking for a specific animal or special information on animal defenses, or if you find a word you don't understand.

SEA CUCUMBER *(Thelemota ananas)*

As the sausage-shaped sea cucumber creeps inch by inch, centimeter by centimeter, across the shallow seabed, it seems like a walking meal. Actually, when it comes to protecting itself from predators, the slow-motion sea cucumber has some very special defenses.

Some species have a poisonous skin to discourage hungry predators. If a predator persists, the sea cucumber tightens its muscles and squirts water from its body. An extremely upset cucumber will turn itself inside out and spew out its innards, including its reproductive and respiratory organs and intestines. The attacker is caught in a tangled mop of organs, and the sea cucumber escapes. It takes about six weeks before the sea cucumber is able to fully regenerate the spewed organs.

Sea cucumbers live in all oceans.

Sea cucumbers are also known as "water pickles." They are very shy critters who like to bury themselves in mud where they are out of a beachcomber's reach.

Wrinkled, flabby, leathery, and punchy as pudding, sea cucumbers are no beauties.

ANIMAL DEFENSES

BURRFISH *(Chilomycterus schoepfi)*

It looks more like a balloon, or a paper sculpture, than a fish! Actually, it is a burrfish in its larval (pre-adult) stage. Many animals go through larval stages—when they look different from their parents—before they become fully mature.

The burrfish is a very close relative of the porcupine fish, but it's a different sort of critter. A porcupine fish will raise its spines and inflate its body with air or water (like a balloon) when it wants to discourage predators. A burrfish, in contrast, is always swimming around with semi-raised spines. Either way, bigger is scarier—and also too much of a mouthful for many predatory fishes.

Fishes aren't the only animals who try to make themselves look fierce. Threat behavior is part of life for many animals. Frogs, lizards, monkeys, and even humans try to look bigger than they really are to avoid dangerous encounters.

There are about 16 species of porcupine fish and burrfish swimming in the tropical ocean waters of the world.

The barbel to feel you with! Barbels are whiskery growths on the snouts of some fishes, and they contain sensory receptors for taste (or smell) and touch.

Pufferfish puff up sideways, not longways! The length of a pufferfish stays the same when it inflates its body, while the width expands like a balloon.

ANIMAL DEFENSES

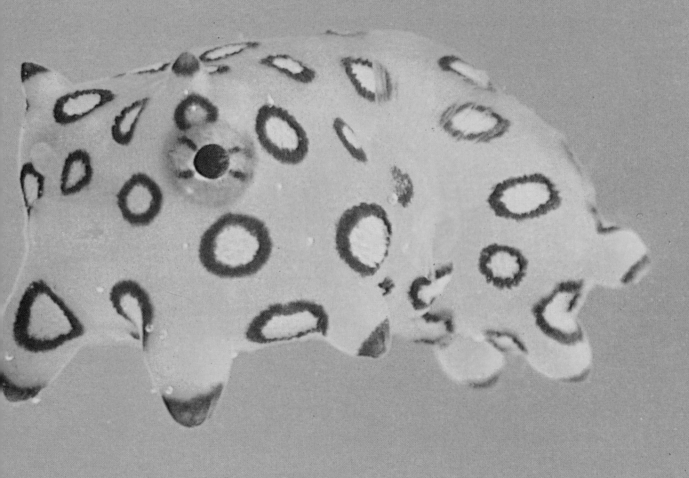

GELADA *(Theropithecus gelada)*

Rough, tough, and hefty, geladas are fierce troopers. The ruff of hair around an adult male's shoulders makes him look even tougher and heftier than his 45 to 60 pounds of muscle. Since these monkeys have come down from the trees to spend most of their lives on the ground, they have developed new ways to defend themselves from predators like lions, hyenas, and especially leopards.

Long teeth, strong jaws, and powerful shoulder muscles provide protection, and organized group defense gives them power in numbers against any common enemy except humans.

Geladas have thick lustrous coats and naked bright red chests. They live at high elevations where food is scarce. Most of their diet consists of grass, roots and all. But they also eat seeds, leaves, onions, and occasional insects—almost anything they can find. Geladas are formidable fighters. To ward off enemies, they will throw stones or roll rocks downhill. Geladas are not fond of their relatives, hamadryas baboons.

Primates are amazingly strong. A 45- pound gelada male has the strength of a human male who is three to six times bigger!

Baboons are close relatives of geladas. Baboons love babies—anybody's! Adults in the troop act as grandparents, aunts, and uncles, sharing food, grooming fur, and cuddling babies in their laps.

Baboon babies have it made in the shade! While grown-up baboons go off to hunt for food, baboon babies spend their time up a tree swinging, climbing, and monkeying around. A few older baboon "baby-sitters" stay behind to look after things. The tree not only makes a great jungle gym to play on but it also keeps babies off the ground and safe from hungry predators.

ANIMAL DEFENSES

ARMADILLO LIZARD *(Cordylus cataphractus)*

The South African armadillo lizard is named for its tough coat of protective scales that look as thick as medieval armor. This slow creature grows to a length of six inches and is especially equipped to defend itself. When threatened, the armadillo lizard puts its tail in its mouth and rolls into a tight ball. This way, predators may get a mouthful of spiny skin, but the lizard's soft belly is protected. The armadillo's layered scales are so thick, they seem as hard as rocks—and not very tasty!

Armadillo lizards are active during the day and spend their time on the ground. Dry ground at that! These animals are found in desert habitats. They can't afford to be particular about how hot it gets or what they eat, and they're not. Over centuries, they've evolved for a perfect fit.

Another armored lizard, the horned toad, lives in North America. When battling with canine or feline predators, this horny creature will squirt jets of blood from its eyes. That could mean a surprise for your cat or dog.

Like horned toads, thorny devils from Australia are ant gourmets. When they find an ant trail, they'll sit and devour the insects for hours.

ANIMAL DEFENSES

Prickly Critter

SLATE PENCIL SEA URCHIN *(Eucidaris tribuloides)*

The sea urchin is a very spiny critter. Beneath its many spines is a globe-shaped exoskeleton (outer skeleton) called a test, made of five plates that are hardened by deposits of lime. While the exoskeleton protects the sea urchin's insides, its outer spines help discourage predators. Spines are also handy to keep a sea urchin on the move. A ball-and-socket joint at the base of each spine is attached to the test by tiny muscles. These muscles tilt the spines and "walk" the sea urchin wherever it needs to go.

Echinoderms are thought to be the invertebrates most closely related to vertebrates (like us!). Zoologists have studied the development of the echinoderm's embryos and have learned that their ancestors were similar to the ancestors of vertebrates.

Sea urchins may also use their spines to burrow into rock crevices and to sting their prey. Many a swimmer remembers the painful sting of an urchin.

There are about 800 species of sea urchins, and they vary in size from two inches to one foot in diameter. The slate pencil sea urchin lives in the waters of the Caribbean and the tropical Atlantic.

Although sand dollars are fuzzily spined and flat, they are related to sea urchins. By the time sand dollars and sea urchins wash up on beaches, they've usually lost most of their spines.

ANIMAL DEFENSES

SOUTHERN RING-NECK SNAKE *(Diadophis punctatus)*

Do you know someone who is scared to death of snakes? Most of us do. Why? Some snakes are deadly and should be feared, but as we've already discovered, most snakes pose no real threat to humans. Why are so many of us afraid of snakes?

Snakes are long, slithery, and silent. They are also secretive, so often they are misunderstood. Snakes have also played the bad guy in myths, folktales, and cartoons. Usually, when people take the time to learn about snakes, they lose much of their fear and gain respect.

Pick up a rock or peer under a log in North America or Central America and you might find a ring-neck snake peering back at you. A ring-neck snake poses no threat to humans, but it has a way of letting you know when it is threatened by you. It hides its head under its coiled body and curls up its tail to show off a rusty or yellowish color on its underside. It may also give off a bad-smelling odor to discourage hungry predators.

These ground-dwelling snakes are named for the yellow or orange ring around their neck. They feed mostly on lizards, salamanders, young snakes, and worms. They kill their prey by constriction. Of course, they don't have to constrict worms.

Scared of snakes? In the United States, you're more likely to die from a lightning strike (and your chances of that are slim!) than a snakebite.

Some fears—called phobias—are not based on reason. They can be hard to get over. Many people have phobias about flying in airplanes or staying in small spaces or about spiders or snakes. Specialists know how to help people overcome their phobias.

ANIMAL DEFENSES

MUSK-OX *(Ovibus moschatus)*

To look at the thick, matted fur of the musk-ox, you might think it's a very old critter. Indeed, this single living species has been around for a very long time. Two-thousand-year-old fossil remains of the musk-ox are regularly found in northwestern Siberia.

Both the male and female musk-ox sport broad, curving horns. The base of the horns almost meets in the middle—something like a Viking helmet.

The musk-ox lives only in Arctic tundra, and it depends on the thick, coarse hairs that cover it from head to hoof to shed rain and snow. A dense inner layer of soft hair serves as insulation to keep frost out.

Musk-ox are sociable animals, and they usually travel in herds of 10 to 20 members (although they may number as many as 100!) in search of food. During long winter months, they eat crowberry, cowberry, and willow. When the weather warms up, they browse on grass and sedges.

Although musk-ox look big and tough, they must defend themselves against predators. To do this, they form a circle (heads usually facing outward) around their young. This is a good form of protection from predators such as wolves but not against humans; entire herds have been destroyed by human hunters.

The musk-ox is named for the musky odor given off by males during the rut, or mating season.

Each summer, adult bulls (males) battle to determine who will be leader of the herd. Their fights last for more than 45 minutes and may include head-on collisions at 40 kilometers (25 miles) per hour. During their battles, they bellow and roar.

ANIMAL DEFENSES

BULLDOG ANT *(Myrmecia gulosa)*

Wasps, ants, and bees, and their relatives, belong to one of the biggest insect groups in the world. There are at least 200,000 known species, and more are discovered each year.

It's easy to spot a member of this group: look for a very narrow waist where the thorax and the abdomen meet. But watch out for the stinger of many female bees, wasps, and ants. The ovipositor (egg-laying organ) at the tip of the female's abdomen can inflict a painful sting, which is used in self-defense.

In addition to a stinger, many ants have fierce jaws that may inflict a painful bite. Members of some species are also able to shoot formic acid from their abdomen as they bite so their unfortunate victim feels double the pain!

The most primitive (those who closely resemble their ancestors) of all ants belong to a subfamily called Ponerinae. The ponerines are the largest, most colorful, and most aggressive of living ants. They include bulldog ants, most of which are inhabitants of Australia.

There are about 100 species of bulldog ants; these impressively large ants may reach a length of one inch (about 25 mm). In addition, they are feared for their aggressive nature and extremely painful sting. This they inflict with a stinger that is one quarter of an inch long. Although many species of ants live in huge colonies of 100,000 individuals, only a few thousand bulldog ants will live together in simple earth nests underground.

Bulldog ants are nimble hunters who prey mostly on insects and spiders, which are fed to the larvae. Adults also have a sweet tooth for the juice of plants. Bulldog ants are pugnacious and will attack anything that disturbs their nest, including humans. They have been known to pursue people for 30 feet, and besides being swift runners, some can leap several inches.

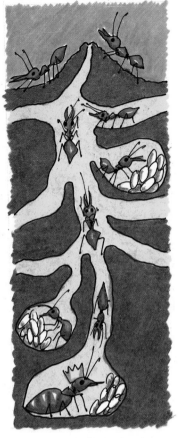

Ants often live in huge colonies (with 100,000 individuals!) in which they communicate by smell and touch.

ANIMAL DEFENSES

AFRICAN PORCUPINE *(Hystrix africaeaustralis)*

This Old World porcupine is covered with blackish quills—very sharp, stiff hairs—banded with white. It also sports a shortish tail tipped with rattle quills that produce lots of noise. When alarmed, this prickly rodent will fan and rattle its spines, stamp its feet, and charge backward in an effort to "stick" its enemy. It has been known to injure and even kill lions, hyenas, and humans.

African porcupines prefer life in deserts, grasslands, and forests in the southern half of Africa. They take shelter in caves, crevices, and borrowed burrows; they also make their own dugout homes, which they line with grass.

Nighttime is the right time to find African porcupines searching for roots, bulbs, and tubers to eat. They may also feed on insects and carrion and gnaw on bones. Although they rarely climb trees, African porcupines are nifty swimmers.

The prickly porcupine's quills may grow to a length of 35 centimeters (more than 13 inches). That's a lot of sticking power.

Old World porcupines run with a shuffling, clumsy gait when they're frightened.

The female African porcupine gives birth to a litter of one to four young, born with open eyes and short, soft quills.

ANIMAL DEFENSES

HOATZIN *(Opisthocomus hoazin)*

A punk-spiked head crest, blood red eyes, and a naked blue face are enough to qualify the South American hoatzin (wahtseen) as a one-of-a-kind bird. But there's more! The hoatzin is one of the few bird species that live mostly by eating leaves. Like a flying cow, the hoatzin digests its food by fermentation in the front part of its gut. Because so much space is taken up for digestion, there's not much room left for flight muscles, and no one looks to the hoatzin for graceful fancies of flight.

Although hoatzins are clumsy when airborne and are prone to crash landings, they are energetic climbers and nifty swimmers. At the first sign of danger, baby hoatzins use a pair of sharp claws on each wing to crawl out of the nest onto thin branches. If predators are persistent, the babies dive from their tree nests and plunge to safety in the water below—sometimes as far as 20 feet below! They swim easily using wings and feet to paddle, and when the danger passes, they climb back up to the nest. To do this, they use their wing-claws and neck to perform bird-like chin-ups.

Hoatzin families are large because young and adult siblings stay around to help breeding parents care for the newest batch of young. Hoatzins feed (or graze) for one to two hours each morning, at dusk, and sometimes even later on full-moon nights.

Is it a bird or a reptile? Wing-claws—claws set on the second and third "fingers" of each wing—are leftovers from all birds' reptilian ancestors. For this reason, hoatzins resemble *Archaeopteryx*, a.k.a. "ancient winged one." Young hoatzins only have wing-claws for the first three months of their lives. After that, the claws callus over.

In the water, hoatzin predators include piranhas and South American alligators.

ANIMAL DEFENSES

SPINED SPIDER

Clinging from the center of its web, the tropical spined spider might easily be mistaken for a wood chip, a flower, or some strange, exotic fruit. This short-legged spider relies on camouflage as well as its tough, leathery abdomen and colorful spines to discourage lizards, birds, and other predators from taking a spiky mouthful. But even sharp spines don't protect these spiders from wasps. Spider wasps sting their victims and carry the bodies back to line their nests. That way, wasp larva have plenty of spider bodies to eat.

Spined spiders use a special decoy to catch fly-eating insects. They decorate their web with little tufts of silk that look like tiny midge flies. When insects stop by for a "fly bite," they are trapped in the web instead.

Male spined spiders are pygmies compared to females. Small size comes in handy for males when they're courting and mating with short-tempered females—they're almost too small to be noticed, or eaten!

Wasps are dangerous to many spiders! Spider wasps are deadly to tarantulas; the big spiders hardly ever survive an encounter with this foe. This wasp crawls into a tarantula's burrow and stings the spider after a fierce battle—both rolling over and over. When stung, the spider is paralyzed. Alive but helpless, the giant spider is dragged to a grave dug by the wasp. The wasp deposits her egg inside the spider's abdomen and fills the grave with dirt. The spider may stay alive for months providing fresh food for the wasp larvae after they hatch.

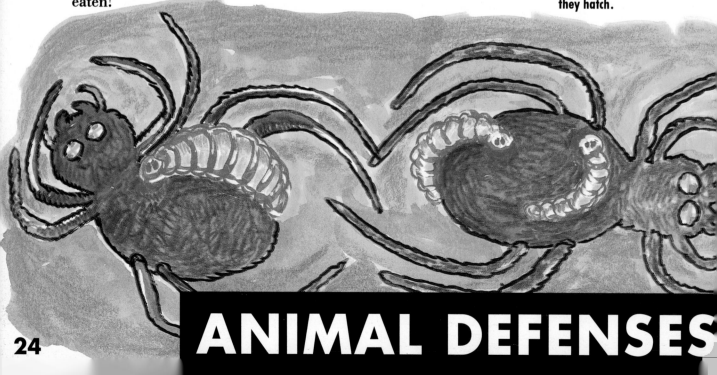

ANIMAL DEFENSES

PLUMED BASILISK *(Basiliscus plumifrons)*

In the rain forests of Central America lives a very distinguished lizard—the basilisk; it can run on water. For this reason, the basilisk is known by local people as the Jesus Christ lizard. Speedy basilisks have been clocked at speeds of 12 kilometers per hour as they whizz across land or water. Because their toes are widened with skin and they run on their two hind legs at such speeds, they don't have time to sink! They are also moving too fast to be caught by aquatic predators.

Basilisks can start their run across water in three ways. They can begin on land, jump onto water from a branch, or rise to the water's surface. You might call them the triathletes of the lizard world.

But basilisks are not content to skim the waves; they also hang out underwater. They are super swimmers and excellent divers, and they can stay on the bottom of a lake or steam for as long as 30 minutes. That's a nifty way to avoid predators on land.

Mythical monster? No, a basilisk. This little lizard is named for a mythical Greek monster who was half rooster and half snake. Supposedly, the monster's looks could kill by turning you to stone!

The skinny! Lizards (and other reptiles) shed their skin at regular intervals. Large flakes and pieces fall off, and a shiny new skin is already underneath. This process is called molting.

ANIMAL DEFENSES

WARTHOG *(Phacochoerus aethiopicus)*

Even with a mouthful of tusks and a hide covered with bristles and warts, there's something debonair about the warthog. Although it is generally mild-mannered, a warthog will defend itself when necessary. Its tusks can cause severe injuries. The big upper tusks look dangerous, but the lower—smaller and sharper—pair do the most damage.

Warthogs live in Africa south of the Sahara Desert, especially where the land is grassy or lightly forested. When grazing, they often shuffle along on their padded wrists. They are usually active during the day, except in areas where they are hunted by humans. Then they come out only after dark.

To raise their young (piglets), and sleep, and hide out, warthogs use natural holes or aardvark burrows. They often live in "clans" of four to 16 members, although adult males usually keep to themselves.

During the mating season, male warthogs do battle with other males. They butt tusks and heads together, and the warts on each side of their head cushion the blows.

When a warthog is relaxed, or munching on grass, roots, berries, or bark, its tail hangs down. On the run, a warthog's tail rises straight up like a wiry flagpole.

ANIMAL DEFENSES

FIREWORM (*Hermodice carunculata*)

Female fireworms are flashy critters; they produce a substance that glows like—you guessed it—fire! When they are not glowing, fireworms are a greenish gold color, and their many parapodia (paired outgrowths from the side of each segment of the animal) are red and white. All fireworms have another hot trick. When humans or other animals touch the fireworm's thick tufted bristles, they get an "on-fire" feeling. This is caused by tiny poisonous, breakable hooks in the bristles.

Fireworms live in sandy Mediterranean seabeds where they create U-shaped burrows. When they are burrowed in, they wiggle their bodies to stir things up and to circulate fresh water. As the water passes over their gills, they extract the oxygen they need to live.

Fireworms are only one species out of 8,000 that belong to the class Polychaetes. All members of this group are segmented worms. Their long bodies are made of many parts, each separated by partitions, instead of joints.

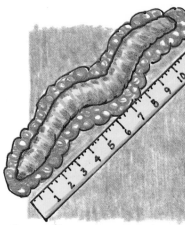

Some fireworms reach a length of 12 inches!

When you're beachcombing, look for the burrows of lugworms. These animals live in U-shaped burrows; telltale signs include two holes several inches apart with a pile of sand next to one.

ANIMAL DEFENSES

This glossarized index will help you find specific information on animals and animal defenses. It will also help you understand the meaning of some of the words used in this book.

African porcupine (*Hystrix africaeaustralis*), 20

Archaeopteryx—the name given to a dinosaur bird species with claws on its wings, 22

armadillo lizard (*Cordylus cataphractus*), 10

baboon, 8

barbels—whiskery growths on the snouts of some fishes that contain sensory receptors for taste, smell, and touch, 6

Basiliscus plumifrons—plumed basilisk, 26

bulldog ant (*Myrmecia gulosa*), 18

burrfish (*Chilomycterus schoepfi*), 6

camouflage—physical appearance that blends in with background, 24

Chilomycterus scoepfi—burrfish, 6

Chlamydosaurus kingi—frilled lizard, 30

coloring, 14, 18, 22

constriction—a method of suffocation some snakes use to kill prey, 14

Cordylus cataphractus—armadillo lizard, 10

Diadophis punctatus—southern ring-neck snake, 14

diet, 8, 10, 14, 20, 22, 28

draco lizard, 30

echinoderm—scientific phylum that includes sea stars, sea urchins, and sea cucumbers, 12

Eucidaris tribuloides—slate pencil sea urchin, 12

exoskeleton—the outer skeleton of an invertebrate, 12

fermentation—a process that allows animals to break down their food for digestion, 22

fireworm (*Hermodice carunculata*), 30

frilled lizard (*Chlamydosaurus kingi*), 30

gelada (*Theropithecus gelada*), 8

group defense—a method of defense that gives animals power in numbers and protects them from predators, 8, 16

habitat—a geographic area where a plant or animal species naturally occurs (all living things have habitats), 10

Hermodice carunculata—fireworm, 30

hoatzin (*Opisthocomus hoazin*), 22

horned toad, 10

Hystrix africaeaustralis—African porcupine, 20

invertebrates—animals that do not have backbones (90% of all animal species on earth), 12

larval stage—immature stage some animals pass through when they look different from mature members of their species, 6, 18

musk-ox (*Ovibus moschatus*), 16

Myrmecia gulosa—bulldog ant, 18

Opisthocomus hoazin—hoatzin, 22

Ovibus moschatus—musk-ox, 16

ovipositor—the egg-laying organ at the tip of a female ant's abdomen, 18

Phacochoerus aethiopicus—warthog, 28

phobia—a fear that is not based on reason, 14

phylum—second-largest taxonomic grouping of all living things

piglet—a baby warthog, 28

plumed basilisk (*Basiliscus plumifrons*), 26

Polychaetes—a class of animals that includes the fireworm, 30

Ponerinae—a subfamily in which all ants belong, 18

porcupine fish, 6

predator—4, 6, 8, 10, 12, 14, 16, 22, 26

primate—highly developed scientific order of mammals that includes humans and monkeys, 8

pufferfish, 6

reptile, 22

reproduction, 16, 20, 24, 28

sand dollar, 12

sea cucumber (*Thelemota ananas*), 4

senses, 6, 18

skin, 10, 30

slate pencil sea urchin (*Eucidaris tribuloides*), 12

southern ring-neck snake (*Diadophis punctatus*), 14

species—narrowest taxonomic grouping of living things, 6, 12, 16, 18, 22

spined spider, 24

sting, insect—the female wasp, ant, and bee can use her ovipositor (stinger) to inflict painful stings, 18, 24

taxonomy—a scientific system to classify all living things

test—the globe-shaped outer skeleton of a sea urchin, made of five plates that are hardened by deposits of lime, 12

Thelemota ananas—sea cucumber, 4

Theropithecus gelada—gelada, 8

threat behavior—physical display animals use to appear larger and fiercer when threatened, 6, 30

tundra—large, cold, treeless land in arctic regions, 16

vertebrates—all animals with backbones, 12

warthog (*Phacochoerus aethiopicus*), 28

webs, 24

young, care for, 22, 28

zoologist—a scientist who studies animals, 12